The Bear Man
A Native American Folk Tale

by Christine Wolf
illustrated by Sheila Bailey

PEARSON

Scott
Foresman

Editorial Offices: Glenview, Illinois • Parsippany, New Jersey • New York, New York
Sales Offices: Needham, Massachusetts • Duluth, Georgia • Glenview, Illinois
Coppell, Texas • Ontario, California • Mesa, Arizona

This folk tale has been told by the Pawnee Indians for many years.

Once there was a young boy who was just like a bear. He walked like a bear. He hunted like a bear. He even slept like a bear.

His people thought they knew why he was like a bear.

Before the boy was born, his father was often away in the woods. One day he found a lost bear cub. It made him think of a child.

Though he was a great warrior, the boy's father was careful with the little bear. He talked to the bear. He gave him pieces of his own food. He even tied some of his own charms around the cub's neck.

"Someday," he told the cub, "I will have a child. If he is ever hurt, I hope he will be taken care of too."

Then the boy's father returned home. He told his wife about the cub. She thought about the little bear. She also thought about the baby she would have.

As the boy grew, he acted like a bear. He played with bears. He even said he could turn into a bear. He was known as the Bear Man.

And he became a great warrior, like his father.

One day the Bear Man's people went to war. All the warriors were killed. Only the Bear Man lived. But he was badly hurt.

Two bears found him. One said, "I know him. He has played with us. He has shared his food with us. We must take care of him."

The bears cleaned him. They gave him water to drink. Then they lay down with the Bear Man. They warmed his cold body.

The two bears fed the Bear Man. They made him well. Then they all went together to the Bear Man's home.

The Bear Man's family was very happy to learn he was alive.

The two bears told the Bear Man to be brave. They told him to be strong. The bears hugged him. Then they were gone.

The Bear Man made up a bear dance. To this day, the children still learn this dance.

Read Together

Today, the home of the Pawnee Nation is in Nebraska and Kansas. The Pawnee people have lived on wide-open lands for over 700 years.

The Pawnee call corn "the mother." They believe it is the most important thing they can grow.

The Pawnee have always hunted and farmed. They grew corn, squash, beans, and pumpkins.

The Pawnee warriors would make their hair stick up like horns. They used buffalo fat and paint on their faces and bodies.

Today, Pawnee Indians do many things. Some are doctors. Some are lawyers. Many work to help others in the Pawnee Nation.